# The Married Man's GUIDE TO CHEATING

---

## RULES AND REGULATIONS OF THE GAME

*Mr. Goodbar*

iUniverse, Inc.
Bloomington

# The Married Man's Guide to Cheating
## Rules and Regulations of the Game

iUniverse books may be ordered through booksellers or by contacting:

iUniverse
1663 Liberty Drive
Bloomington, IN 47403
www.iuniverse.com
1-800-Authors (1-800-288-4677)

Because of the dynamic nature of the Internet, any Web addresses or links contained in this book may have changed since publication and may no longer be valid. The views expressed in this work are solely those of the author and do not necessarily reflect the views of the publisher, and the publisher hereby disclaims any responsibility for them.

Any people depicted in stock imagery provided by Thinkstock are models, and such images are being used for illustrative purposes only.

Certain stock imagery © Thinkstock.

ISBN: 978-1-4502-7816-4 (sc)
ISBN: 978-1-4502-7817-1 (ebk)

Library of Congress Control Number: 2010918820

Printed in the United States of America

iUniverse rev. date: 2/14/2011

# Stop!

## Warning!

This book is sensitive to the female touch so, if you are female and continue turning the pages of this book it will self-destruct!!!!

5!

4!

3!

2!

1!

# Contents

All right! All right! You got me—but there is a sniper watching you, so I wouldn't continue turning pages of this book if I were you! Okay, enough. I was just having a little fun, but thank you for purchasing this book. I hope you enjoy reading it at least half as much as I enjoyed writing it.

# Introduction

Variety is the spice of life! Can you imagine what life would be like without variety—only eating soup every day, watching only one television show, or wearing the same shirt or pair of pants every day? Doesn't that seem ludicrous? So why would we have sex with the same person for the rest of our lives? Don't get me wrong. Marriage can be good—even great at times— but it can also get to be repetitive, which leads to boredom.

This book was written to try to help you enjoy the spices of life without having to pay the ultimate price. By that, I mean alimony, child support, or losing half of your possessions. Since most of the knowledge in this book comes from married men that have been successfully cheating and married men that have been caught cheating, you will get a lot of valuable insights as to what you should do when cheating—as well as a lot of great insights and what you shouldn't do when cheating. Just about every married man that I've asked how long he has been married has given the same answer: "Too long!"

Since they haven't learned how to explore or taste the different spices of life—or they're feeling bored or trapped and they're looking for a way to release—they don't know how to go about doing it. I hope that the contents of this book can help them out of their monotonous, mind-numbing relationships. I have been in a happy and successful marriage for more than fifteen years because I know the secret to longevity. Keeping a marriage fresh is being able to have your cake and eat it too. The majority of the men that *don't* cheat are only faithful out of fear of being caught—not because they don't want to. I bet that if you asked one hundred men whether they would cheat if there were no way that they could possibly get caught, 99 percent of them would say "Hell yeah!" in a heartbeat!

This book is in no way, shape, or form telling you to go out and cheat, but it gives you some tips and pointers if that's what you decide to do. Remember that you're an adult—so don't blame me for your infidelities or the choices you may make after reading this book. Play at your own risk!

# Chapter 1:

## The Potential Mistress

Women. Believe it or not, most married men don't just go out looking to have an affair—especially a long-term affair—but sometimes it just happens. An occasional one-night stand maybe, but sometimes we get into a steady, ongoing relationship with another woman—and that's when everything changes.

Sometimes what we think is going to be a harmless one-night stand or just a friend with benefits for a while can turn out to be a long-term, ongoing affair. One of the main reasons for this is that usually the people that we have affairs with are the people that we already know or the people that we have encounters with on a regular basis—whether it's a coworker, a friend, a friend of a friend, or even a friend of the wife! I know that sounds dirty, but those types of situations happen all the time.

Since most of these women are already aware that they are about to get involved with a married man, they should already know to keep all of their emotions in check, right? Wrong!

Even though they are aware of the situation that they are about to get into, they still can't help getting emotionally involved—and the longer the affair goes on, the worse it gets. That's where all the problems start—so there are rules to dealing with a potential mistress.

**Rule #1: Any woman that you get involved with should know that you're married**.

Any woman that you get involved with should always be aware that you are married. Once you let her know that you're married, you're placing the ball in her court—and then it's *her* decision to pursue it or leave it alone.

Timing is everything on this one because if you spring the "M" word on them too quickly, it can turn them away. However, once they get to know you a little better and your personality starts to grow on them, they start to feel comfortable around you. It almost becomes okay for them to get involved with you—even though they know that you're a married man. Once they get into that comfort zone, flirting seems to become harmless banter and exchanging numbers doesn't seem like such a big deal anymore. As a matter of fact, flirting with her and being married can be something of an aphrodisiac to her—and they make you even more desirable in her eyes. I guess that's just human nature. It seems like the things that we can't or shouldn't have are the things that we want or desire the most. I guess it is the old Adam and Eve forbidden fruit syndrome.

Any woman that's willing to get involved with you knowing that you're married is probably just looking for the same fun-filled, physical, no-strings-attached relationship that you are.

I can't even begin to fathom having a mistress and not being able to sleep with her. That's like having a Lamborghini and not being able to drive it—what's the point? So she's definitely in it for all of the same reasons that you are. Any woman that's willing to be your mistress is most likely willing to be your (insert fantasy here) chick as well, which brings me to rule #2.

**Rule #2: Never wait until after you've had sex with the other woman to let her know that you're married.**

Waiting until after you've had sex with the other woman to let her know that you're married is just asking for drama. Even if you've never denied being married or it never even came up in a conversation, she will still feel hurt and used, as if you've lied to her. "Hell hath no fury like a woman scorned!" You don't want that type of drama in your life—especially if she knows where you work or the kind of car that you drive!

One way or another, all of my married buddies and I have had to learn this lesson the hard way. I will never forget my first time stepping out in my marriage. The woman that I was involved with (let's just call her "Snickers") caught me cheating on her—with my own wife! Yes, you read that right—it wasn't a typo.

I wanted to get involved with this woman, but she knew that I was married and wanted no parts of that. Since she was thicker than a Snickers and I wanted her bad, I lied to her and told her that my wife and I were separated and weren't in a sexual relationship anymore.

You're probably thinking that I'm such a dog and that I was dead wrong. Yeah, I know—but shut up! If you had seen her, you would have done the same thing—so don't judge me! We started vigorously dating, but I was successfully hiding the fact that I was still married.

One day, my wife and I were walking together holding hands at the South Florida Fair and we walked right in front of Snickers! She looked at me in shock as if she was about to walk over to us and say something. I guess she thought twice about it—or maybe she really didn't want to deal with the confrontation—but she chose not to say anything. I'm glad that she didn't because I don't know what I would have done in that situation. I'm sure that I would have said, "Baby, I don't know this crazy bitch"! Either that or I would have punched her in the face and yelled, "Run! She has a bomb!" What other choices would I have had?

Somehow she let me go that night. I thought that she would let me off the hook and that would be the end of it, but I was wrong. She didn't let me get away unscathed—she made me pay for it later. She flattened my tires and keyed the word "Liar" into the passenger side of my car! I couldn't really get mad because I knew I deserved it. I took it with a grain of salt and sucked it up.

Flattening tires, busting out windows, and keying up cars must be in the "Women That Have Been Wronged" handbook.

I learned that costly lesson the very first time that it was taught to me—and I don't ever want a refresher course. I guess that old saying is true when they said "no pain, no gain." Now I'm straight up with women when it comes to matters of the heart, and they can either take it or leave it. If it's meant to be, it'll be. I just sit back and let nature take its course.

Since most women perceive sex to be the beginning of a relationship, you should always volunteer that information so that there are no mishaps or misunderstandings later on down the road. I think I speak for all men when I say that none of us wants to deal with the head-rolling, finger-pointing, "Let me tell you about yourself" attitude when we're presenting you with an indecent proposal. We do not need to hear any of those dreaded clichés—"All men are alike," or "Men are such dogs," or the worst one of all "Oh no you didn't." When we're trying to pursue a "jump-off."

There's nothing you're telling us that we don't already know. Just go with the flow or step politely to the left and *shut up*—or at least do your bitching elsewhere. Thank you very much.

**Rule #3: Never lead her to believe that the relationship is more than what your intentions are.**

If you're only keeping the other woman around for sex, then she should be aware of that. Let her know that her share is just physical—and it could be over at any given time.

That's where a lot of guys go wrong. You should never be leading the other woman on, thinking that you may be moving in with her or leaving your wife for her—if those really aren't your intentions.

Even if you intend to leave your wife for her, you still shouldn't let her know that—you should just wait until it happens. If you tell her that you're going to leave your wife, she's going to become anxious and bothersome, wondering when she's going to get her chance to become the number one lady in your life. That's nothing but a headache and an argument waiting to happen. You know whether or not you're just keeping her around to fulfill your sexual needs—so why lie to her? Why play games and lead her to believe something that's not true? People get hurt when they play with people's feelings—and playing with a woman's feelings can get you a quick trip to the emergency room.

What you're doing is building problems for yourself and causing confusion. One lie leads to another lie and another lie and another—you can only go on for so long before those lies catch up to you. You have to be real and honest with her from the very beginning and everything else should just fall into place. The only thing that you should have to worry about is the home front, which brings me to my next rule.

## Rule #4: Don't change when you start getting strange.

Strange is a term of endearment that we use to describe having sex with new people. Never change your habits or mannerisms when a new piece of ass comes into the picture. You set off all kinds of bells, whistles, and red flags at home when you start changing your habits. Don't stay out all night with the guys if you used to always be home in time for dinner. Don't start grooming well if you wouldn't shave for a funeral before. Don't buy new clothes if you were known for wearing the same pair of jeans for a week straight. By the way, shame on you if you've done any of those things.

Those telltale signs will set off a woman's intuition. Don't think for one minute that your wife isn't taking mental notes about what's happening. She just hasn't said anything yet because she's building a case against you like the DEA. She's waiting until she has enough evidence before she swoops in and takes you down. Don't let the possum trick fool you. Staying on your toes will always keep you a step ahead of the game—and two steps further away from the courtroom.

I act fidgety and restless. Sometimes I go out for a drive as if being cooped up in the house is getting to me. This little habit of irregularity makes it easy for me to slip away at random times without raising alarms or arousing suspicions.

Randomness is the shield that will keep the bullshit at bay when you're stepping out or "creeping." Having a hobby away from the wife is also a great way to keep suspicions low. Playing in a band and going to practice every day will definitely get you a lot of free time without raising much suspicion. Whatever it is, be consistent. With all of that being said, I'll repeat, "Don't change when you start getting strange.

**Rule #5: Always use protection with the other woman.**

Some men feel as if we can confide in the other woman. We start to develop a bond with the other woman and start putting too much trust into her, but you should never trust the other woman completely—especially when it comes to sex.

A cheater is a cheater. There is a good possibility that if she'll cheat *with* you, she'll probably cheat *on* you. As a local dj here in West Palm Beach, Fl always says (Mark McCrazy x102.3fm) I.J.S." I'm just saying".

Always be wary of the player being played—even if you feel as though you can trust her. If she constantly says, "You're the only one I'm sleeping with," you should still always use protection with her—regardless of what she's telling you. I know this all sounds like common sense, but when we start thinking with our dicks, common sense usually goes out the window. A good friend of mine who is married had a woman on the side. One night they got drunk together, had sex, and he didn't use any protection. For weeks and weeks, he was more nervous than a whore in a church. Every married man that I know with a woman on the side who has gone in without using protection felt the same way.

The big picture is that you have to always protect yourself and your wife from any sexually transmitted diseases. It would be kind of hard to explain an STD or, even worse, a woman showing up at your house with a newborn baby that looks exactly like you! If you're rich and famous, it's much worse. All of the women I know say, "They'd better pull out or I'm keeping it!" Bitches! Always keep your head in the game and remember that it is a game. Losing that game could cost you for a lifetime! Follow the rules and stick to the script and you will have stories to tell your friends while smiling instead of crying.

# Chapter 2:

---

# Know When to Hold 'Em

Every once in a while, we find that one woman that we want to keep around for a while. Maybe we are lacking something at home—or maybe it is their mental support, the way they treat us, or the fact that the sex is just that damn good!

There are two types of women when it comes to mistresses: "pressure cookers" and "teamsters." Some are in it for themselves, have no respect, and could not care less about your happy home or whomever they may hurt in the process. These women are pressure cookers because they could blow your cover at anytime.

This is the kind of woman that knows you have a lot to lose and will use that to her advantage in an almost "don't piss me of or I'll blackmail your ass" sort of way. She wants you when she wants you and needs you when she needs you. She will act like a fool if she can't have her way. She will probably go as far as to disturb your home life to get her way.

There are some unwritten rules of adultery. "Never disturb a married man's home." It's just something that you don't do—

period! At that point, a man feels as though he has nothing else to lose and will defend the home front until the end. Women, don't say that you haven't been told because you've just been warned. Act crazy at your own risk!

When you start to get involved with a woman like that, drama is always just right around the corner. But, when you find a teamster—a woman that's truly down for you—there is no better feeling in the world. Make sure that she is someone who you really want to be with—not just the "I'm-married-so-I'll-take-what-I-can-get" type. You're not shopping for a car—don't just pick based on practicality or what you think you can afford. Pick something that you wanna play with a lot! If you're a breast man, go after the top-heavy melon-monger. If you're an ass man, shop based on trunk space. At some point, that relationship is gonna become work, so make sure it's worth it. In other words, nailing your wife's ugly sister because she's an easy target is a situation that you're almost sure to regret. A teamster is on your team 100 percent and wants nothing more from the relationship other than to be there for you. She knows where she stands in the relationship and won't step out of line—even when she feels like she's getting the short end of the stick—because she knows exactly where her place is. She is the type of woman that you've got to keep on your team for a while—well, at least for a little while.

I've heard people ask why some women can stay with a married man for months—or even years! I'll tell you how. The women that stick around for long periods of time as the other woman only want half a man. They don't want the full experience or responsibilities of a real relationship, such as being tied down or having someone to answer to on a daily basis. She only wants the occasional dates and the occasional sex—all while enjoying her freedom and leaving his wife at home to clean up behind him.

Most of these women get a thrill out of sneaking around with a married man because of the adventure and the always-present danger of being caught. She thinks that it's exciting to have an affair with a married man and will do anything within her power to keep it going for as long as she can—as long as it's fun.

The type of woman I'm talking about does everything that you ask, does everything that you wish your wife would do, doesn't ask questions, is always there when you need her, treats you like a king when you're together—and can suck a golf ball through a keyhole.

She is the type of woman that likes to shower you with gifts, loves to stroke your ego, shows you how much she appreciates you, and believes everything that you tell her—or at least pretends to. She can come face-to-face with your wife and doesn't get rattled, acting as if you don't even matter. She can even hold a conversation with your wife and your wife is none the wiser. A true teamster is my kind of girl!

You've got to keep a woman like that on your team for a few reasons. She's a marriage life preserver—when things feel like they're sinking, your life preserver brings you right back to the top.

I can't tell you how many times that has helped me out in my repetitive, redundant, monotonous marriage. Variety is the spice of life—and it can damn sure keep a relationship fresh and exciting. It can even make fifteen years of marriage seem like nothing. She's the type of woman that you've got to keep on your team—well, at least for a little while.

# Chapter 3:

## Keeping Wifey in the Dark

Keeping your wife in the dark can be a difficult task because you're always playing keep away, trying to keep any incriminating evidence from getting into the wrong hands.

Women are nosy—especially wives. They always want to know what you are doing. *Where are you going? Who are you going with? How much do money do you make? When do you get paid?*

Wives should always be kept on a need-to-know basis. If she doesn't need it, she doesn't need to know it. Too much information gives her the upper hand, which brings me to my first rule to keeping the wife in the dark.

**Rule #1: Keep wifey on a need-to-know basis.**

Never let your wife get the upper hand. Always answer a question with a question. When she starts getting nosy, start getting just as nosy right back at her.

They're only asking you questions that they think they already know the answers to. Answering questions will get you caught up in lies. If you never answer any of her bullshit questions, she can never say that you've lied to her.

Your wife doesn't need to know how much money you're making because if she knows how much money you're making, sooner or later she'll also want to know much money you're spending—and how much of that money is spent on her and where is the rest of it going.

Your wife knowing how much you're bringing in per pay period leads to nothing but problems. When they start asking you how much money you make, watch out. The only reason that they want to know how much money you're making is so that they can try to make plans with your money.

Be careful of questions such as "So how much did you get paid this week?" You can almost see her calculating in her mind how much money she is going to spend at Macy's. She wants to know whether you will still be able to cover her bills.

**Rule #2: Never have any incriminating bills mailed to your home.**

Any incriminating bills should be mailed to a P.O. Box—never to see your home. Credit card bills, phone bills, and bank statements can get you caught—especially if you have a nosy wife—because they display too much information about your current activities.

## Rule #3: Never use joint bank accounts.

Joint bank accounts are for suckers! I bet that your wife is always the one suggesting that you get a joint bank account, right? It's a trick! She's nosy and wants to know everything that is going on. She's trying to pull the wool over your eyes. Don't fall for that! You have to stay firm and stand your ground with this one. No matter how many times she throws it up in face—just say no!

She'll keep tabs on everything that's spent and question you about every little thing that you do. It's nothing but a problem waiting to happen. That's just another way that women try to control you—and everything else in their circle.

## Rule #4: Get your alibis straight.

Never tell your wife that you're going somewhere with someone if they don't know that they are supposed to be with you. If they don't know that they're supposed to be your alibi, it will always come back to bite you in the ass.

Never say that you're going somewhere if they can prove for a fact that you haven't been there. You have to be smart when creeping. Common sense can go a long way. Get your alibis straight—before you start lying. Don't get caught off guard.

## Rule #5: Leave no paper trails.

Sometimes we want to spoil the woman that's taking care of our special needs—or at least try to show her a good time. When you're out with the other woman and you're spending, try your best to only use cash. Cash is always the best way to go because it leaves no paper trails.

Try to refrain from using credit cards or bank cards—they're nothing but trouble. If you must use a credit card, there are prepaid credit cards that leave no paper trails.

## Rule #6: Keep a low profile.

The best way to not get caught cheating is to keep a low profile. You've got to stay out of sight and out of mind—that's why I have a thirty-mile rule. The thirty-mile rule means never doing anything that can be detrimental to your marriage within thirty miles of your home base. I never go to any hotels, shops, or restaurants with the other women within thirty miles of my home.

Some men get so used to cheating that it becomes routine. Almost every man that gets caught cheating gets caught because he has gotten too comfortable and too relaxed in his relationship with the other women. He almost forgets that he's cheating and starts doing stupid things, which leads me to Rule #7.

## Rule #7: Never let down your guard.

You've got to mind your P's and Q's if you want to stay out of the courtrooms, keep your family together, and keep your money in your pockets. You've almost got to keep a worrisome kind of spirit to maintain your relations and not get caught slipping with the other woman. I had to help a buddy of mine move all of his stuff out of his house because he let his guard down and got too relaxed with the other woman. He did something stupid that got him a one-way ticket to Divorce-ville! His wife caught him creeping with the other woman on his birthday. Happy Birthday! The other woman wanted to take him shopping for his birthday and, out of all places, they went to the Palm Beach Mall. Now, I don't know what he was thinking—no, scratch that, he *wasn't* thinking.

I know I'm not the smartest guy in the world, but I know I wouldn't fall for the old "I-want-to-take-you-shopping-for-your-birthday" routine just to be seen with me. If she wants to buy me something for my birthday, I would just have to write out a list for her of the things that I want—or she would just have to pick something out for me.

When we hear the phrase "take you shopping," we just throw all caution to the wind. We're thinking about how much money she's about to save us on those new pair of Jordan's, Nike's, or those alligator skin boots that we were going to buy when we got the chance. Yee Haw! Let me get back to telling you what happened to Rick—oops, I didn't mean to say your name. Sorry, Rick.

After they finished shopping for what he wanted, she wanted to visit Victoria's Secret. When they walked into the store, lo and behold, his wife and her friend were there too. His wife was trying to surprise him with some new lingerie for his birthday. I guess the surprise was on her. Happy birthday!

I wish I could have been there for that one. I would have loved to have seen the look on his face—no, better yet, I would have loved to have seen the look on *her* face! I know he wishes that I had written this book a little bit sooner—he *and* Tiger Woods!

## Rule #8: Always do a clean sweep.

After the other woman rides in your car, you always have to do a clean sweep. Women love to leave stuff behind in your car. I don't know whether it's on purpose or accidental, but they all do it—all of them!

It could be a comb, a brush or something as senseless as a pair of panties (come on, ladies, how do you forget your underwear?), but they always seem to leave something behind. I'm sure that most of them do it on purpose—out of spite—to get back at you for something you've done or because they think that getting you caught up with your wife will bring you and her closer. Whatever the reason, it's just plain selfish and evil. Shame on all of you bitches that do that shit!

To make sure that you're not dealing with that type of woman, you've got to search your car well—no lazy searching. Don't twist your head back and look around while you're driving! Stop! Pull your lazy ass over get your fat ass out of the seat and give it a good search. Don't be a lazy fool.

## Rule #9: No soap showers.

When you're with the other woman and you're supposed to be out working, there is no reason that you should be coming home smelling like a fresh-soaped shower. Any smells that you have on you should come off with just water. It really works. I've been using that technique for years and it hasn't failed me yet.

If you can't get her smell off with just a water shower, then maybe you need to leave that nasty whore alone. Either that or get her a good douche! I.J.S!

## Rule #10: Never volunteer information.

"How was your day, honey?" Women often ask simple questions like that just to find out a little bit about what's going on with you. Any reply should be short and simple. You should simply reply "great" and throw it right back at her. "How was your day, honey?" Always keep the focus on her—they love that.

Women can't get enough of talking about themselves—and that takes the focus off of you. As long as she is hearing herself talk and you're at least pretending to listen, she will think that you and she are sharing some bonding conversational and quality time together. Make sure that you at least pretend to listen.

# Chapter 4:

## Saying "I Love You"

After you've been with the other woman for a while and you're starting to develop some feelings for her, never let her know that you're feeling this way. Once she knows that you're feeling a certain way about her, she might start feeling as if maybe one day she can get you to leave home—or maybe she'll expect you to spend more of your time with her. Either way, it's a bad idea.

Women are emotional creatures. You must constantly remind them of what type of relationship they're in because they are emotionally driven. Most of the time they let their emotions take over logic. There are still some crazy women out there that still think that getting pregnant will keep a man around. *If I get pregnant, he has no other choice than to be with me.* Ha—silly women!

You've got to be careful of what you say to women because they are quick to try to take the relationship to the next level. Never say "I love you" to the other woman—it could cause a catastrophic ripple effect in the relationship.

I know that sometimes we can get caught up in the moment and those three words can just fly out of our mouths—especially during sex—but you've got to learn to control that reflex.

I made that mistake once before when I was naive and inexperienced, but I guarantee you that it'll never happen again.

One night when I was supposed to be out clubbing with the guys, I was in a hotel with the other woman—and I was truly giving her the business! I'm talking about a hair-pulling, ass-smacking, pillows-and-covers-all-over-the-floor, I-hope-they-don't-call-the-police-on-us type of event.

I was about to reach the point of ecstasy and I expressed to her that I was feeling this way—if you can understand where I'm coming from (no pun intended). Before I could reach that sweet point of ecstasy, she stopped, dropped, and inserted my love tackle (Mr. Goodbar) into her mouth. She began to express her love for me in a way that only a mother could be proud of!

I was getting the best head of my life. I swear it was magical. I think I saw pink hearts, yellow moons, blue diamonds, green clovers, and purple horseshoes. Before I knew it, I shouted, "Damn, girl, I love you!" It was a bad move, but I wasn't thinking at the time. She caught me in a vulnerable state of mind and I didn't know what I was doing. Ladies, if a man tells you that he loves you during sex, it's not him talking. It's his penis talking—he's not thinking with the right head.

All of the blood has left his brain and he's in no position to make any type of remarks or decisions that should be taken seriously. What we're really trying to say in those moments is: "I love your pussy, not you." Don't take that to heart and run with it.

At that moment, I was trying to say, "I'm in love with your mouth," but it just came out wrong (no pun intended). I got caught up in the moment and lost my couth.

Listen, women, no man should be held accountable for anything that he says or does in that moment of weakness. You should just take them as sweet nothings and let it go. Although, ladies, it *is* a great time to ask your boss for a raise. Ha!

She took my moment of weakness seriously and ran with it. That was the beginning of the end for us. She started calling me more than usual and showing up unannounced where she knew I would be. She was getting emotional about every little thing. Even worse, I think that after that night, she felt as if I was obligated to spend more time with her. The nerve of that bitch! She was trying to take over and become the main lady. She knew what it was from the beginning, but that didn't stop her from trying anyway.

Saying those three horrible words changed everything and left me with no other choice than to let it go.

# Chapter 5:

## Know When to Fold 'Em

Knowing when to fold them is all about signs. There will be a lot of obvious signs telling you that it's time to fly the coop before things get out of hand. Whether or not you choose to ignore or heed those warning signs is entirely up to you, but be warned that choosing to ignore the warning signs can be a costly—even fatal—flaw on your part. Sometimes we see the signs, but choose to ignore them because the other woman is satisfying most of our needs. We tend to let little things slide for a while when we should have nipped it in the bud and checked it at the point of impact.

We say, "Oh, she's just having one of those moments right now. She'll be all right." If you don't check her and her attitude right then, it won't get any better. As a matter of fact, it will only get worse with time—and that was just a preview of what's to come if you choose to ignore it and stay with her.

I was at the barbershop the other day and the barber told a story that amazed everybody—including me. My eyebrows raised and my mouth opened wide. It was so outrageous that I asked him if I could share his story. He gave me the go ahead so I can tell you this story.

My barber and his other woman were at an upscale restaurant. As they were about to order dinner, he got a phone call that changed the complexion of the entire night. He reluctantly answered, spoke a few words, said that he would have to call them back later, and hung up. As soon as he hung up, his mistress wanted to know who he was talking to. She said that she had heard a woman's voice on the other end and demanded to know who it was.

Keep in mind that this is the other woman—not his wife—and she started accusing him of cheating on her. (Yes, you read that correctly.) She started to cause a scene in the restaurant. She was so loud that it embarrassed him, and he begged her to calm down before they kicked them out, but the damage had already been done. When he looked up, all eyes in the restaurant were on them. He told her that they should leave and discuss it further in the car, but she wouldn't hear it.

In an attempt to imitate Mary J. Blige, she slapped him and let him have it as if she was his wife! Right there in the restaurant, he cocked back and "Chris Brown-ed" his irate mistress and she hit the floor like a sack of rocks. He grabbed his things and headed for the door, but she was right behind him—and still talking. She told him that she was not going to be stupid for him anymore and that she was going to start having plenty of men calling her. He told her not to get in his car and that she should find another guy to take her home, but she started to get in the car anyway. He said, "Don't get in my car!" and started pulling her arm so that she wouldn't get in.

At the top of her lungs, she yelled, "Help! Help!" Finally, he said, "Fine—just get your stupid ass in the car and let's go." He pushed the back of her head to the point where her face hit the car. When he started to walk around to the driver's side, she followed him. She was highly upset that he had pushed her face into the car. He hurried up, jumped in the car, and closed and locked the doors. He felt relieved that she was locked out of the car, but that wasn't the end of it.

He pulled away, but he felt her pounding on the back of the car. In actuality, she was doing something else. She was tugging on his license plate because she knew that it could be easily removed. As he was pulling away, she snatched the license plate off the back of his car. When he glanced in his rearview mirror, he saw her holding the license plate and talking on the phone. She was giving the police all of his information. He slammed on the brakes and turned around. He knew that if he didn't go back, he would have been pulled over before he could say, "Officer, I swear I didn't know."

If that wasn't a telltale sign to get as far away from her as possible and leave her the hell alone, I don't know what is! As farfetched as that story sounds, I swear that it's exactly how the story was told. The most absurd part is that he got back with her and she just recently had a baby with him! Yeah, I know—crazy, right? That's definitely the type of woman that you've got to let go of—and let go of in a hurry!

Women are such emotional creatures that they sometimes have a hard time trying to separate those emotions from a physical relationship. Even though everything is out in the open and they are aware of their situation, sometimes they still can't help getting their emotions involved and becoming emotionally attached to a married man. Once her feelings for you become genuine and she starts falling in love with you, that's usually the beginning of the end. That's the point when she starts thinking and doing crazy things that she thinks will keep you around—or, even worse, what she thinks may make you want to leave home to be with her. She starts trying to show you that she has more to offer and that she's a better choice than the woman that you already have at home.

There are always signs that a woman has reached that point in the relationship. When she is ready to advance, you'll know the signs when you start see them. As a man, I know firsthand that—even when we see the signs—we still have to have everything spelled out for us. So, without further ado, here are the signs to knowing when to let go:

**Sign #1: When she can't accept her role in the relationship anymore.**

Some women that you date for a while start getting tired of being number two and feel ready to be number one. Be careful of that type of woman—they're a Lifetime Original Drama waiting to happen. You've got to know what kind of woman you're dealing with and look for the signs before it starts getting out of hand. She'll start dropping little hints. "Are you ever going to leave your wife?" "When are you gonna leave your wife?"

These are telling signs that you should watch out for and you should take effective action immediately. Once that type of questioning starts, you've got to put her back in her place immediately. You have to reiterate what type of relationship she is in, that she knew what this was from the beginning, and that she shouldn't try to change things now because she is getting a little emotional.

There are always questions to look out for that will let you know that she's not content being number two anymore and she's ready to advance the relationship:

- Why can't we go out more?
- If I satisfy all of your needs, why won't you leave home?
- Aren't I better in bed than your wife?
- Am I prettier than your wife?
- We make such a good couple—shouldn't we be together?

All of the above questions should be answered in the same manner—"I've got to go"! She's setting up you up for a fight and you should just leave it alone before it starts. She's just giving you a preview of what's to come. Once those types of questions start, that's your cue to fall back and exit stage left as soon as possible.

**Sign #2: When she starts demanding too much from the relationship.**

Every man knows that there's no such thing as a completely satisfied woman, but some women will pretend to be satisfied— at least for a little while to try to be polite. Sooner or later, she'll grow out of it. When she grows tired of being polite, you'll find out that there's nothing that you can do that will completely satisfy her—no matter how hard you try.

If you give her a diamond, sooner or later, she'll want a bigger one. If you buy her a car, sooner or later, she'll want to trade it in for a better one. So why do we try? I think we all know the answer to that. The answer is the greatest thing ever put on this earth: vagina!

Her "golden box" gives her a lot of room for abject behavior while she's undergoing her improvement stages. The tighter the golden box, the more shit we're willing to put up with—or ignore—for a longer period of time.

Just about everything they do is good at first. Women, you've got to understand that, after a while, your golden box becomes just like a bank to us. Every time we make a withdrawal, we lose a little interest. It's not long before we grow tired of the abject behavior. The little things that didn't bother us before—or that we thought were cute—suddenly become annoying. We no longer want to put up with the pouting when she wants to have her way or the whining when she wants something from you. Those are all the little annoying things that we let slide in the beginning when we're still in pursuit of the golden box.

# Chapter 6:

---

# Breaking It Off

Breaking it off is always a delicate situation. One wrong phrase or word can be the difference between walking away unscathed and getting your head busted open. The weaning process makes all the difference in the matter. Ripping it off like a bandage is not always the best solution to this problem. Nobody appreciates being cut loose and dumped, so there should be a weaning process involved. It all depends on how long you've been fooling around with her and/or how well you know her.

No matter how you say it or do it, some women just will not go with the flow of the program. These women are bitches! Some women will force you to be brutally honest or just downright nasty with them, but—with that approach—you'll just have to take all the emotional drama that comes along with it. Although I believe that honesty is the best policy with the other woman, I also believe that you've got to have a certain amount of couth. There are certain ways that you should go about doing this.

People *say* that they want to hear the truth, but people don't *really* want to hear the truth. It's sort of like trying to tell someone that they have bad breath. If you have any couth at all, you wouldn't just blurt out "Damn, what've you been eating? Shit sandwiches?" No, you would offer them a piece of gum or a mint, right? You can be subtle and still be direct and honest without all of the hostility or aggressiveness. This will definitely help to cut back on all of the drama associated with breaking it off with someone.

I know you're thinking, "She's just the other woman and I don't owe her explanations," but being harsh and making her feel as if you're intentionally trying to hurt her could make all the difference in whether she tries to hurt you back. If you play your cards right, you may even be able to have a good friend and/or an occasional sex partner for life. After breaking it off with previous women, I have still managed to keep a friendly relationship with every single one of them. That's saying a lot, considering the nature and the history of women not taking being dumped lightly or maturely.

I'm the guy friend that they call on when they need a guy's opinion, someone to confide in, or a shoulder to cry on. I'm also that guy friend that she calls when your relationship isn't going that great and she still needs an occasional maintenance job. That's one of the reasons that—even though I'm married—I've still managed to stay "coochie rich" for so long. I'm just saying! We all know that, most of the time when we break it off, it's because we don't want anything to do with that person anymore, right? Sometimes we're just getting tired with the current situation and need a change of pace or we're getting tired of the woman and need a change of strange.

Not that she's necessarily done anything wrong, but sometimes the same old pack of crackers can get stale and we just want out of the current situation. Here are some rules to follow when you're trying to breaking it off cleanly with the other woman.

**Rule #1: Wean them.**

Your first step to breaking it off with the other woman is to stop making yourself so available. Always being available when she calls is not going to help your case at all. You've got to make her feel as though she's also tired of being in the relationship with you. Do things that are unattractive or aggravating to her that will start to make her wonder why she is even wasting her time. When you completely break it off with her, she will feel as if it was a mutual separation. Also, no sex—period! You cannot—and I repeat, cannot—want to break it off with the other woman, but continue to have sex with her. That's not going to cut it. As much as we would like to have our cake and eat it too, it just will not work in this case. You are sending mixed signals and you will bring confusion into the situation once you try to break it off with her. You will have to leave "Big Willie" in the holster—at least until she has completely moved on. Just as she perceived sex to be the beginning of a relationship, she will also see it as a notion that you are on good terms and are getting back together. You've got to use your big head on this one—not your little one, dummy.

**Rule #2: It's never her fault**.

Remember that—no matter what—it's never her fault. It's always your fault as to why you want to break it off. "It's not you—it's me. I'm feeling guilty about this whole thing and I just want to be faithful to my wife now." Even after all of that, some women just can't let it go. After you've broken it off and she still refuses to let it go, you've just got to do what you've got to do to make sure that she gets the message. When all else fails and she knows you want to break it off—but she's still not quite ready to let it go—you've got to bring out the big gun. God! You've got to let her know that you've realized that what you are doing is wrong in God's eyes and you can't live like that anymore. Let her know how sorry you feel about the situation and that you just want to move on and put your sins behind you. There are very few people out there that will question God and they should get the message loud and clear. It seems so wrong, but when honesty doesn't work and you want to break it off peacefully, you've got to do what you've got to do.

Thankfully, I've never had to go to that extreme. Usually the other woman and I have a good understanding and they know that when it's over, it's over. She's free to roam because, as long as we're together, she is not allowed to have any relations with anybody else. It might sound crazy, but that's the way that it has to be. She knows that as long as we are together, all of her needs will be met and taken care of. However, as soon as we are over, she knows that all birthday gifts, dates, and favors are off.

# Chapter 7:

## Getting Caught

I always hear people say that men get caught cheating more than women because men are stupid. Well, while I believe that to be partially true, I don't think that's always the case. I think that men get caught cheating more than women do because men deal with women and women deal with men. A man can cheat with a married woman and no one would ever know—except maybe her best friend—because he's not going to let his emotions get involved and ruin what he has. He's just happy to be getting some on the side. The best part about it is that, when he's done with her, he gets to send her back home to her hubby and no feelings ever get involved. Women messing around with married men almost always have to get their feelings involved or try to upgrade to number one and try to take over wifey's spot. The big difference between men and women getting caught cheating is feelings.

Just about every player in the game of adultery eventually gets caught. A running back in football can only get handoffs for so long before he eventually fumbles. It is playing against the odds—and the odds are that you will get caught eventually. You've got to play it more like a boxing match: stick and move, stick and move. Remember what I said about routine? Players get caught when they start to get into a routine.

Getting into a routine will get you caught up like a mosquito in a bug zapper, a bear in a trap, a fish in a net, or a deer in the headlights. Once you get caught cheating, you have to keep your composure and be smart. There are only two rules to follow when getting caught. How you get caught decides which rule you should follow.

**Rule #1: Deny, deny, deny!**

If you're not caught cheating red-handed, then you have to deny, deny, deny. Have you ever heard Shaggy's song "It wasn't me"? I couldn't have written a better song myself. Don't admit to anything—you've got to try to make her think that she's crazy and everything that she's talking about is ludicrous. So what if she found a number in your pocket? Rip it up in front of her and let her know that shit was nothing! So what if she found a stain on your sheets? Let her know that you had personal moment with yourself and she missed out—she should have been there. No matter what, if she didn't catch you in the act, then you've done nothing wrong and she can't prove anything. Don't let her accuse you of doing anything if she doesn't have cold hard evidence to support her case. Tell her to find something better to do with her time. Turn around and walk away to let her know that you're not worried about the shit she's talking about—or run to avoid catching a one-two to the back of the head!

You know your woman—and you know what you can and what you can't get away with. You've got to stand firm with this issue—even when she's standing there with her mean mug on and her fist balled up about to Mary J. Blige you. You have to stand firm as if you've done nothing wrong. You've got to keep a serious look on your face that says, "I don't know what your problem is, bitch, but you'd better calm down." Women can smell guilt a mile away so, even when you're staring directly into the face of divorce, you *can't* lose your composure. Remember that guilty is as guilty does—so if you're not acting guilty, then maybe you're not guilty. Right? If she values your relationship, it won't take long before she'll start questioning her actions and wondering whether she was overreacting. Nothing in this rule applies to you if you've been caught red-handed. Obviously, once you've been caught red-handed, all deniability goes out the window and you're in a whole new ballgame (no pun intended). If you get caught red-handed, you don't have many options, so you've got to roll with rule #2.

**Rule #2: Apologize!**

When you've been caught with your hands in the cookie jar, you don't have a whole lot of options. Your first option should be to duck or run—or both simultaneously. Saying you're sorry should work most of the time—or maybe after things have cooled down a little bit. I think that most women know or believe that infidelity is not the end of the world—or even the end of the relationship. Although she may want to kill you at that moment, with a little time, there's a good chance that she will forgive you under most circumstances.

You can try to turn it all around on her and play "Billy Bad Ass" and tell her that it's all her fault that she caught you cheating—that's right, her fault! It's all her fault that she caught you in that bed with that other woman—maybe she didn't show you enough affection. It's her fault that she caught you in Victoria's Secret with that other woman! Of course I'm being facetious. I wouldn't advise any man to do that to any woman in that situation. What other choice do you have besides saying sorry or blaming her for your infidelities? Getting caught is probably the worst experience that you will ever have to endure during a marriage—and that pain won't just go away over night. Even when she has taken you back and says that all is forgiven, she has never forgotten. I think that it can sometimes make a marriage better and stronger. I think that it helps both parties realize how much they mean to each other. You shouldn't grow complacent in your marriage and stop doing all of the things that you were doing when you first got together because there is always somebody out there that is willing to step up to the plate and fill that void. Love is the most powerful thing on earth and, if it's true love, infidelity shouldn't come between that—no matter how big a ho your husband is!

# Chapter 8:

## Up Your Game
## (Written by Hoggerello)

Affairs are about excitement, bragging rights, and—most importantly—satisfaction. You might have pulled the sexiest thing since (insert fantasy here), but you have two, maybe three bad performances before she drops your ass.

Bringing something to the table that she's always wanted and never even knew existed is the best way to maneuver another woman into the position of "Keeper." I had one chick who knew nothing about herself until after I came along. When we met, she was all business: get together, do the do, kiss on the cheek, and roll out. It was not a bad relationship, but it was definitely not the kind you talk about with your friends on the ride home.

Go into every extramarital situation the way you would go into a fistfight you have your plan, but you're also paying attention, listening, watching, seeing what works, what doesn't, and what you should never do again. If you get knocked out as she puts a foot on your neck and steps on your feelings—never do that again!

Your woman will involuntarily tell you with her sound effects and body language what works, what doesn't, and how well...Pay attention! The sex part of this thing is not solely for your pleasure if you treat it like it is, not only are you going to find yourself unable to keep a mistress but you're also going to take one more potential mistress off the market for those of us who know what the hell we're doing, ya selfish bastard! There is a reason that only virgins were sacrificed because hoes are a necessary part of life—don't fuck it up for everybody.

The ability to change up your routine and bring multiple techniques to the bedroom or car or kitchen is the surest way to keep her where you want her (knees or back, whatever) and the best way to ensure that she keeps coming back for more. If she's a real keeper, she'll start doing her homework to satisfy you as completely as you satisfy her.

Once you've done your homework, look the part and get your mind right. The only thing left to do is enjoy, but not too fast. Women who have been satisfied by you are much more forgiving of a bad performance. The first time is where legends are born!

If you start off slow and get better over time, she *will* believe she's training you and will expect you to become the keeper. But if you knock her socks off right out of the gate, she will fall into a comfortable submissive position that she'll have no problem getting comfortable in and staying in.

Remember that control of the situation is your responsibility. You have the most to lose she needs to know her role in your life and she needs to enjoy it.

# Summary

---

Women, just because your man steps out on you occasionally doesn't mean that he doesn't love you. It doesn't mean that he's not still a good man or that you're not a good wife. Sometimes men just need to feed their egos and sometimes we feel that conquering women is the best way to do that.

No man wants to intentionally hurt his woman, but unfortunately that's what usually happens when we play our games. Sometimes we've got to get off the train to get back on track and realize what's really important to us. Forgiveness is the best gift you can give someone after they've done something wrong—plus life is too short to hold grudges. Do yourself a favor—either let it go or let them go. You'll live life a whole lot better! Peace!

www.ingramcontent.com/pod-product-compliance
Lightning Source LLC
Chambersburg PA
CBHW020403290526
45785CB00005B/2421